Brown Bear

The Biggest Meat-eater on Land

by Meish Goldish

Consultant: Kerry Gunther
Bear Management Office
Yellowstone National Park

BEARPORT
PUBLISHING

New York, New York

Credits

Cover, © Christian Riedel/Shutterstock; TOC, © Suzann Julien/iStockphoto; 4, Kathrin Ayer; 4–5, © Andy Rouse/The Image Bank/Getty Images; 6, © Dieter Hawlan/iStockphoto; 7, © Oksana Perkins/iStockphoto; 8, © Lynn M. Stone/Nature Picture Library; 9, © Robert Sabin/Animals Animals Enterprises; 10L, © Erwin & Peggy Bauer/Animals Animals Enterprises; 10R, © Andrej Štojs/iStockphoto; 11, © age fotostock/SuperStock; 12, © John Shaw/Photo Researchers, Inc.; 13, © Wildlife GmbH/Alamy; 14, © Alan & Sandy Carey/Peter Arnold Inc.; 15, © age fotostock/SuperStock; 16, © BostjanT/iStockphoto; 17, © Stouffer Productions/Animals Animals Enterprises; 18, © Leonard Rue Enterprises/Animals Animals Enterprises; 19, © Matthias Breiter/Minden Pictures; 20, © Yva Momatiuk & John Eastcott/Minden Pictures; 21, © Sergey Gorshkov/Minden Pictures; 22L, © M. Watson/Arden; 22C, © age fotostock/SuperStock; 22R, © David Courtenay/Photolibrary; 23TL, © Erwin & Peggy Bauer/Animals Animals Enterprises; 23TR, © Stouffer Productions/Animals Animals Enterprises; 23BL, © Yva Momatiuk & John Eastcott/Minden Pictures; 23BR, © Stouffer Productions/Animals Animals Enterprises; © 23BKG, Robert Plotz/iStockphoto.

Publisher: Kenn Goin
Senior Editor: Lisa Wiseman
Creative Director: Spencer Brinker
Original Design: Otto Carbajal
Photo Researcher: Picture Perfect Professionals, LLC

Library of Congress Cataloging-in-Publication Data

Goldish, Meish.
  Brown bear : the biggest meat-eater on land / by Meish Goldish.
    p. cm. — (More supersized!)
  Includes bibliographical references and index.
  ISBN-13: 978-1-936087-25-9 (library binding)
  ISBN-10: 1-936087-25-1 (library binding)
  1. Brown bear—Juvenile literature. I. Title.
  QL737.C27G65 2010
  599.784—dc22

                          2009029849

For more information, write to Bearport Publishing Company, Inc., 101 Fifth Avenue, Suite 6R, New York, New York 10003. Printed in the United States of America in North Mankato, Minnesota.

102009
090309CGA

10 9 8 7 6 5 4 3 2 1

Contents

Beary Big

The brown bear is the biggest meat-eating animal on land.

An adult brown bear standing on its back legs is nearly as tall as a basketball hoop!

Brown bears can grow to stand about 9 feet (2.7 m) tall. They may weigh up to 1,500 pounds (680 kg). Males are bigger than females.

5

An Outdoor Home

Brown bears live on mountains, in forests, and by rivers in parts of North America, Europe, and Asia.

During most of the year, they live outdoors and sleep on a bed of grass or leaves.

They usually make their homes where people don't live.

Most North American brown bears live in Alaska and Canada. Some, however, live in parts of Wyoming, Montana, Idaho, and Washington State.

Brown Bears in the Wild

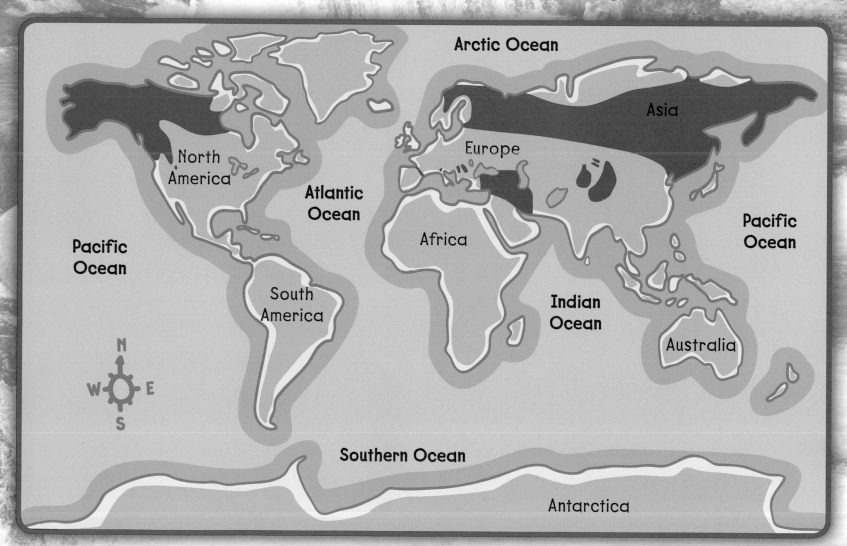

Arctic Ocean

North America

Atlantic Ocean

Pacific Ocean

South America

Europe

Asia

Africa

Indian Ocean

Pacific Ocean

Australia

N
W E
S

Southern Ocean

Antarctica

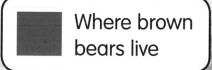

Where brown bears live

Colorful Names

Brown bears are named for the color of their fur.

Some bears, however, may be dark brown, while others are a light cream color.

Still others have such dark fur that they look black!

In the United States, brown bears are also called grizzly bears because the fur on their backs is streaked or "grizzled" with gray.

In Alaska, brown bears are also called Kodiak bears. Brown bears, grizzly bears, and Kodiak bears are all the same kind of bear.

Fast and Strong

hump

Brown bears are strong and quick.

Their shoulders have a large hump, which is a bundle of muscles that gives them great power.

A brown bear is so strong that it can knock down a tree by pushing and pulling at it with its front paws.

It can also run as fast as a horse for short distances.

claws

Brown bears have five strong, sharp **claws** on each paw. Each claw is about as long as a person's finger.

Powerful Hunters

Brown bears are powerful hunters.

Yet they usually don't attack people unless they feel they're in danger.

When a brown bear stands up on its back legs, it may seem like it's about to attack.

However, the bear just wants to get a better look at its surroundings!

Brown bears usually live alone. They do spend time with other bears when they mate or when they are raising their young.

Bear Foods

Brown bears eat other animals such as mice, fish, deer, and moose.

They also use their sharp claws to dig up roots and to grab nuts and berries off trees and bushes.

In fact, many brown bears eat more plants than meat.

They also love to stick their faces into hives to eat the honey that bees make.

Kodiak bears are the largest kind of brown bear. They grow so big because they eat salmon, a fish that has lots of fat.

Planning for Winter

Brown bears **hibernate**, or sleep, throughout the winter in **dens** that are dug either into the side of a hill or under a tree.

The bears get ready for their long sleep by eating as much food as they can in the summer and fall.

The food gets stored in their bodies as fat.

The bears live off the fat during the cold, snowy months when they are asleep.

Brown bears usually don't hibernate with other adult bears. Females will hibernate with their young, however.

Having Babies

Before brown bears hibernate, they mate in May or June.

Around late January or early February, the female bear has one to four babies called **cubs**.

The mother gives birth while she sleeps!

The cubs drink her milk, even though she is asleep, for about three months.

ten-day-old cubs

At birth, a brown bear weighs only one pound (454 g).

Growing Up

In the spring, the bears wake up from their long winter nap.

Then the mother teaches her cubs how to hunt for food.

She keeps them safe from enemies such as wolves and mountain lions.

She also keeps her cubs away from their own father, who might try to eat them!

By age two or three, the cubs are big enough to start life on their own.

Brown bears live for about 25 years in the wild.

More Big Bears

Brown bears are one of seven kinds of bear in the world. They belong to a group of animals called mammals. Almost all mammals give birth to live young. The babies drink milk from their mothers. Mammals are also warm-blooded and have hair or fur on their skin.

Here are three more big bears.

American Black Bear

The American black bear can weigh up to 650 pounds (295 kg).

Andean Bear

The Andean bear can weigh up to 340 pounds (154 kg).

Sloth Bear

The sloth bear can weigh 310 pounds (141 kg).

Brown Bear:
1,500 pounds/680 kg

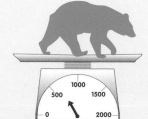

American Black Bear:
650 pounds/295 kg

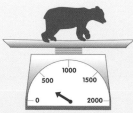

Andean Bear:
340 pounds/154 kg

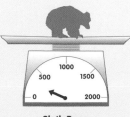

Sloth Bear:
310 pounds/141 kg

Glossary

claws (KLAWZ) the hard, sharp, curved nails found at the ends of the fingers or toes of an animal

dens (DENZ) the homes of wild animals

cubs (KUHBZ) baby bears

hibernate (HYE-bur-nate) to spend the winter in a deep sleep

Index

Read More

Barnes, Julia. *The Secret Lives of Brown Bears*. Milwaukee, WI: Gareth Stevens (2007).

Gibbons, Gail. *Grizzly Bears*. New York: Holiday House (2003).

Legg, Gerald. *Bears*. New York: Franklin Watts (2007).

Learn More Online

To learn more about brown bears, visit
www.bearportpublishing.com/MoreSuperSized